Along the ALASKA HIGHWAY

PHOTOGRAPHY BY ALISSA CRANDALL

TEXT BY GLORIA J. MASCHMEYER

ALASKA NORTHWEST BOOKS™

ANCHORAGE . SEATTLE

Library of Congress Cataloging-in-Publication Data
Crandall, Alissa.
    Along the Alaska Highway / photography by Alissa Crandall ; text by Gloria J.
Maschmeyer.
        p.   cm.
    Includes bibliographical references (p. 91) and index.
    ISBN 0-88240-410-5
    1. Alaska—Description and travel—1981- —Guide-books.   2. Alaska
Highway—Guide-books.   3. British Columbia—Description and travel—1981- —
Guide-books. 4. Yukon Territory—Description and travel—1981- —Guidebooks.
I. Maschmeyer, Gloria J.   II. Title.
F902.3.C67   1991
917.9804'5—dc20   91-16263
                                                                         CIP

Edited by Anne Halloran
Book design and cover design by Elizabeth Watson
Photo editing by Carrie Seglin
Maps by Elizabeth Watson and David Berger

PHOTO CREDITS: All photos are by Alissa Crandall except the following:
The Anchorage Museum of History and Art, page 13. U.S. Army Corp of Engineers,
1.14, 17. South Peace Historical Society, 15. Edwin Bonde, 16. Special Collections
Division, University of Washington Libraries, 19. B.C. Archives and Records
Services, 33. George Johnston Tlingit Indian Museum, Teslin, Yukon, 45. George
Johnston Tlingit Indian Museum, Teslin, Yukon, Yukon Archives-Whitehorse, 57.

Alaska Northwest Books™
A division of GTE Discovery Publications, Inc.
22026 20th Avenue Southeast
Bothell, WA 98021-4405

Printed in Singapore

Preface

November 1992 marks the fiftieth anniversary of the Alaska Highway. Once, only a hardy few traveled its rutted course. Today most of the road's rugged twists and punishing surfaces have been tamed, but its mystique remains undiminished. *Along the Alaska Highway* was created not only to commemorate the birthday of this remarkable thoroughfare, but also to celebrate the vivid world through which it passes.

The perfect companion to The MILEPOST®, Alaska Northwest Books' guide to western Canada and Alaska, *Along the Alaska Highway* speaks to both the armchair voyager and seasoned traveler. To create their photo essay, Alissa Crandall and Gloria J. Maschmeyer have drawn upon a wealth of Alaska Highway experiences. Their images offer intimate glimpses of the rhythms of the roadside, where natural splendor meets striking individualism. Whether a journey on this exhilarating route is planned or simply dreamt about, *Along the Alaska Highway* is a call to adventure.

— The Editors of **Alaska Northwest Books**™

ACKNOWLEDGMENTS

I am grateful to my parents, who taught me I can accomplish anything I set my mind to. I'd also like to thank everyone else, especially Gloria Maschmeyer, who helped me incorporate what were once just ideas into a book.

From much earlier travel, I had already learned what also applies to the Alaska Highway: the journey is what matters, not the destination.

What I didn't know was the generous extent to which highway residents would respond to this project, nourishing us with food and friendship. Even during the busy tourist season, they took time to share stories about life along the roadside. I will especially remember the home-baked goodies of Loryne Andrews and Ellen Davignon, and the help of Danny and Uli Nowlan, and Ollie Wirth.

Special thanks to Lee Damron, who let us put 10,000 miles on his new camper before he even got to use it himself.

And thanks, too, to the raven. I met him when he woke me up at 7:00 one morning as he was pecking insects off my windshield. He reminded me that the joys of the Alaska Highway aren't always expected, and they come in all sizes, large and small. — A. C.

Few accomplishments are achieved by a single person, and so it is with this book. My appreciation goes to my partner Alissa Crandall, who had the idea and laid the groundwork for my field research. I am grateful for her persistence, perseverance, and faith in me.

To those along the Alaska Highway who opened their doors and hearts to us, my sincere appreciation. Thank you Mary Hansen, Chaddie Kelley, Andrew Isaac, Joyce McNutt, Doug and Rita Euers, Donna Bernhart, Walter Northway, Ollie Wirth, Charles Eikland, Betty and Ed Karman, Bill Brewster, Orval and Helen Couch, Alan Fry, Beth Phillips, Ellen Davignon, Watson Smarch, Jake Melnychuk, Dennis and Joey Froese, Jack Gunness, Loryne Andrews, George and Mary Behn, Winnis Baker, Dorothy Rutherford, Gary Loiselle, Lee Damron, and countless others. Your generosity and enthusiasm helped fill this book with the spirit of the North.

Special thanks also go to the team at Alaska Northwest Books™—Maureen Zimmerman; Sara Juday; Jerianne Lowther; Kris Valencia; editors Anne Halloran and Ellen Wheat, who went beyond the call of duty to meticulously edit the final manuscript; and the design team who beautifully pulled it all together.

I also thank my family: my in-home editor and oldest daughter Ingrid, whose confidence in me is unfaltering; my encouraging teenagers Adam and Erika; and finally my husband, Dick, whose support helped make his wife's dream a reality. — G. J. M.

RIGHT: FALL'S COLORS ILLUMINATE THE ROADSIDE NEAR KLUANE LAKE IN THE YUKON TERRITORY.

PAGE 8: THE SURFACES OF THE ALASKA HIGHWAY ARE CONTINUALLY BEING IMPROVED, MAKING IT ACCESSIBLE TO ALL KINDS OF VEHICLES.

CONTENTS

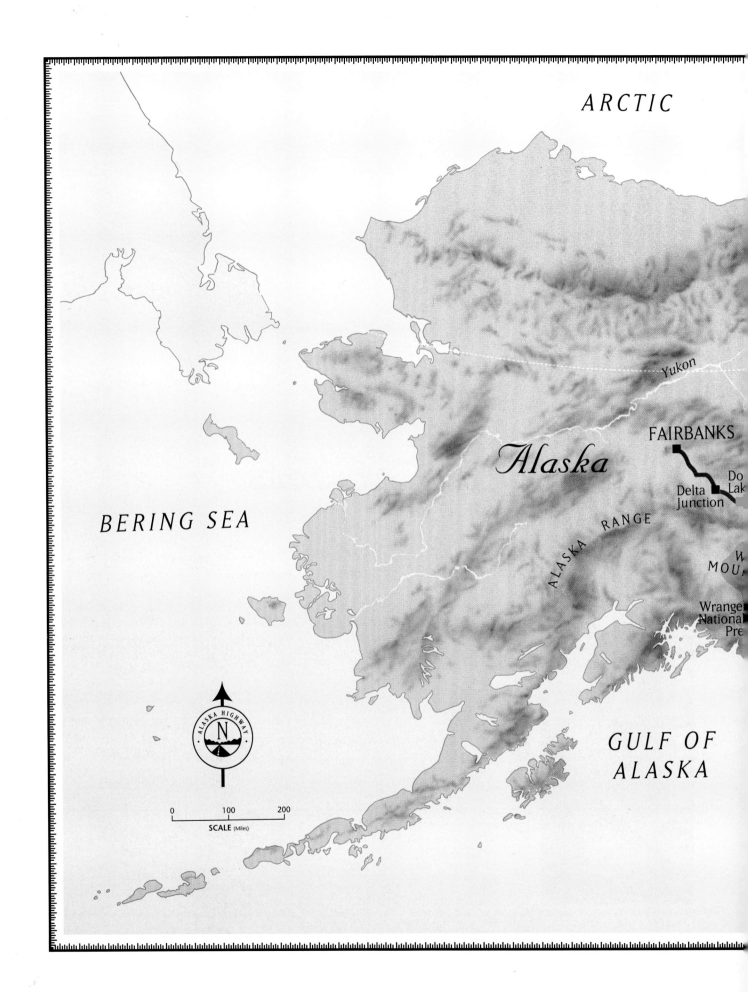

ARCTIC

Alaska

BERING SEA

Yukon

FAIRBANKS

Delta
Junction

Do
Lak

ALASKA RANGE

W
MOU

Wrange
National
Pre

GULF OF
ALASKA

N

ALASKA HIGHWAY

0   100   200
SCALE (Miles)

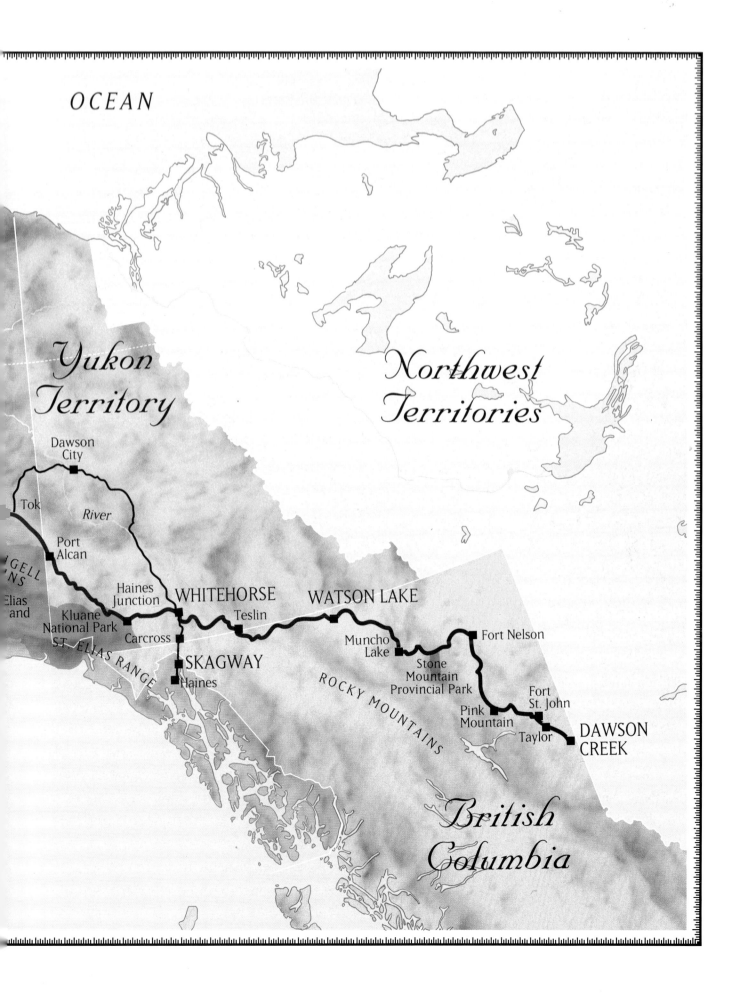

OCEAN

Yukon Territory

Northwest Territories

Dawson City

Tok

River

Port Alcan

IGELL
NS

Elias
and

Haines Junction

WHITEHORSE

WATSON LAKE

Teslin

Kluane National Park

Carcross

SKAGWAY

Haines

ST. ELIAS RANGE

Muncho Lake

Fort Nelson

Stone Mountain Provincial Park

ROCKY MOUNTAINS

Pink Mountain

Fort St. John

Taylor

DAWSON CREEK

British Columbia

A WILDERNESS JOURNEY

One-half century ago, the Alaska Highway cut a swath through the wilderness, linking the territory of Alaska to western Canada and the United States. Today, many of its early hairpin turns have been straightened and most of its washboard surface has been smoothed by asphalt. But improvements haven't diminished the excitement of the highway. It remains an adventure, crossing some of the most remote landscapes in the world.

Incomparably beautiful, the route passes through rolling farmland carved out of raw wilderness. Jagged mountain ranges appear like mirages on the horizon. Pristine lakes turn up with dazzling frequency. At night, the sky comes alive. Northern lights dance, and an occasional shooting star explodes into space.

Wildlife flourishes here. Mountain ridges are home to Dall and Stone sheep. Valley floors host meandering moose and bear. Bald eagles soar overhead, silhouetted against bright blue skies, and snowshoe hares bound across the roadsides into profusions of wildflowers.

Since the road's construction in 1942, thousands of people have made their way north from Dawson Creek, British Columbia, to Delta Junction, Alaska, the official end of the highway. Take your own journey along the Alaska Highway, the great road north.

LEFT: THIS MODERN STRETCH OF ROADWAY NEAR DOT LAKE IN ALASKA IS TYPICAL OF MUCH OF TODAY'S HIGHWAY. *RIGHT:* LABORERS CUT A PATH THROUGH THICK FORESTS OF SPRUCE, PINE, AND OTHER TREES TO CREATE THE ALASKA HIGHWAY.

THE MAKING
OF THE ROAD

LEFT: WORKERS MIGRATED
FROM ALL OVER THE UNITED
STATES AND CANADA TO
PARTICIPATE IN THE
CONSTRUCTION OF THE
HIGHWAY. THE ROAD CREWS
OFTEN TOILED 16 HOURS A DAY,
7 DAYS A WEEK.

RIGHT: IN THE 1940S, RAIN
TRANSFORMED SOME SECTIONS
OF THE ALASKA HIGHWAY INTO
AN IMPASSABLE MIRE. SOME
UNLUCKY VEHICLES REMAINED
STUCK FOR A MONTH.

The idea of an overland route connecting Alaska and northwestern Canada to the United States wasn't new in March of 1942, when construction of the Alaska Highway began. Both countries had long toyed with the notion. Whatever reservations existed were quickly overcome when Pearl Harbor was bombed and the United States entered World War II. Suddenly, Alaska assumed strategic significance.

While the road never became the military supply lifeline its proponents envisioned, it was a stunning accomplishment. During the somber time of war, U.S. engineers carved a 1,500-mile highway through the wilderness. The project consumed the energy of 11,000 soldiers and countless civilians, and was completed in only eight months. The pioneer route was dedicated on November 20, 1942.

Most of the money to pay for the $138 million project came from the United States, which also supervised the construction work. Less convinced of the road's military importance, Canadians deferred to the Americans' greater enthusiasm. They agreed to the project with the understanding Canada would assume control of its part of the highway after the war. Led by the U.S. Army Corps of Engineers, firms from both nations carried out the work. Civilian laborers included Natives and trappers, who were invaluable as guides.

The road took its general direction from the Northwest Staging Route, a chain of Canadian commercial airfields begun in the 1930s. Eventually reaching from Edmonton, Alberta, to Fairbanks, Alaska, the staging route cut across the Canadian prairies. During the war, the airfields were used as part of a lend-lease program providing military supplies to Russian allies. Aircraft and materiel were shipped to Russian crews waiting in Fairbanks.

The road's many twists and turns continue to inspire romantic speculation. Some contend the highway was built crooked to discourage the possibility of an enemy air attack. Others maintain the meandering was the logical result of "sight" engineering: surveyors guided the road's direction with compasses from the tops of vehicles. Another interpretation is simply practical: the highway followed the most solid ground.

Construction of the road began in Dawson Creek, British Columbia, then the northern terminus of the Northern Alberta Railroad. The other end of the highway was Delta Junction, Alaska, where it connected with the Richardson Highway heading north to Fairbanks. Crews started work from both ends, their camps established at 100-mile intervals. Almost immediately, engineers and workers faced unprecedented challenges. Attempting to cut through the wilderness with bulldozers and Caterpillars, road crews found their progress frequently blocked by rivers and streams. Ferries and portable pontoon bridges were hurriedly created; eventually 8,000 culverts and more than 100 bridges were assembled.

Vast stretches of permafrost (permanently frozen subsoil) and muskeg (pockets of decayed vegetation) were another hurdle. When tampered with in the process of road building, these areas turned into seas of muck, sometimes leaving operators no choice but to abandon their machinery. To cover the swampy areas, a layer of rough-cut logs was laid down. Called corduroy, this time-consuming method was very effective and is still in use today.

Burdens were perhaps most keenly felt by individuals on the road crews, some laboring 12 to 16 hours a day, seven days a week. Suffering temperatures ranging from 90 degrees above zero to 70 below, several perished from exposure. During the summer they were plagued by mosquitoes and other pests. Housing was primitive, consisting of tent camps. As with those who came to place the trans-Alaska pipeline 30 years later, steady wages and high adventure compensated many workers for the hardships. At $1 an hour, the pay seemed good for those who had been sidelined by the Depression.

RIVERS AND STREAMS OFTEN BLOCKED THE WORKERS' PASSAGE, REQUIRING THE HURRIED CREATION OF OVER 100 BRIDGES.

For the communities located along the route, the project resulted in a prosperity not seen since gold rush days. Local vendors struggled to keep up with the human influx. Post offices accustomed to receiving 50 pieces of mail a week were suddenly deluged with thousands. Women took in laundry, baked bread, and cooked meals for the workers. And residents along the highway opened their homes to overnight visitors. Longer lasting benefits included the infusion of facilities built by the Army and the technical expertise the engineers offered. In Fort St. John alone, the Army added a waterworks and a movie theater.

No sooner had the road been dedicated than work began in earnest to upgrade it with a gravel bed. Private companies were awarded the majority of contracts, and the U.S. military gradually withdrew. What was informally known as the Alcan Highway was officially named the Alaska Highway in 1943. In 1946, Canada's portion of the road was officially turned over to the Canadian government, and civilians became the major users of the road in the late 1940s.

Tourists who travel the highway each year still find frost heaves on the northern stretches, and road crews occasionally frustrate their passage with construction. But the romance of the highway burns as brightly as ever.

MUSKEG BOGS THAT COULD TRAP EQUIPMENT IN SEVERAL FEET OF MUCK WERE A CONSTANT CHALLENGE TO HIGHWAY ENGINEERS.

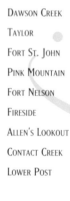

dged by islands and adorned throughout by mountains and cobalt blue lakes, British Columbia has been spectacularly blessed. Canada's westernmost province is larger than any state in the United States except Alaska, and within her borders lies an enviable bounty of resources and wildlife. With most of British Columbia's three million residents clustered in the cosmopolitan centers of Vancouver and Victoria, 90 percent of this magnificent land remains unpopulated, a remote, pristine wilderness.

Native peoples thrived amid thick forests and plentiful fishing grounds. For 12,000 years the Kwakiutl, Cowichan, Sooke, Haida, Tsimshian, and others fashioned complex cultures and vivid art; the mysterious totem pole is among their legacies. On the heels of white explorers' awestruck accounts came the miners and prospectors. Captain James Cook took sea otter pelts from the lush shores of Vancouver Island, then introduced them to a covetous world. Soon afterward, fur-trading posts crisscrossed the region.

In the middle of the nineteenth century, thousands of outsiders braved the steep canyon enclosing the Fraser River, lured by the call of gold. Settlers followed the traders and prospectors, most from the British Isles. The Chinese came to work on the railroad, the Japanese to fish and farm. British Columbia's cultural fabric has

LEFT: FALL FOLIAGE BURSTS INTO A KALEIDOSCOPE OF COLOR NEAR THE SETTLEMENT OF LOWER POST, B.C.

ABOVE: TSIMSHIAN TOTEM POLE.

always been rich, enhanced by trade with distant countries.

Few regions ever possessed such abundance to share. Coastal forests—huge with stands of Sitka spruce, hemlock, and cedar—yield lumber. The earth contains minerals of all types, including copper, coal, zinc, silver, asbestos, and nickel. There are at least 600 species of wildlife. North America's largest populations of grizzly, cougar, wolf, and mountain sheep live here. Fast-running streams hold the mountain whitefish. In the far northern waters swim the arctic grayling, walleye, and northern pike.

The Alaska Highway runs through the northeast part of British Columbia, the last major area in the province to be settled. Here, colorful groves of aspen, birch, and willow stand out from the roadside's usual dark forests. From the billowing grainfields of the Peace River valley, the highway rises, heading north.

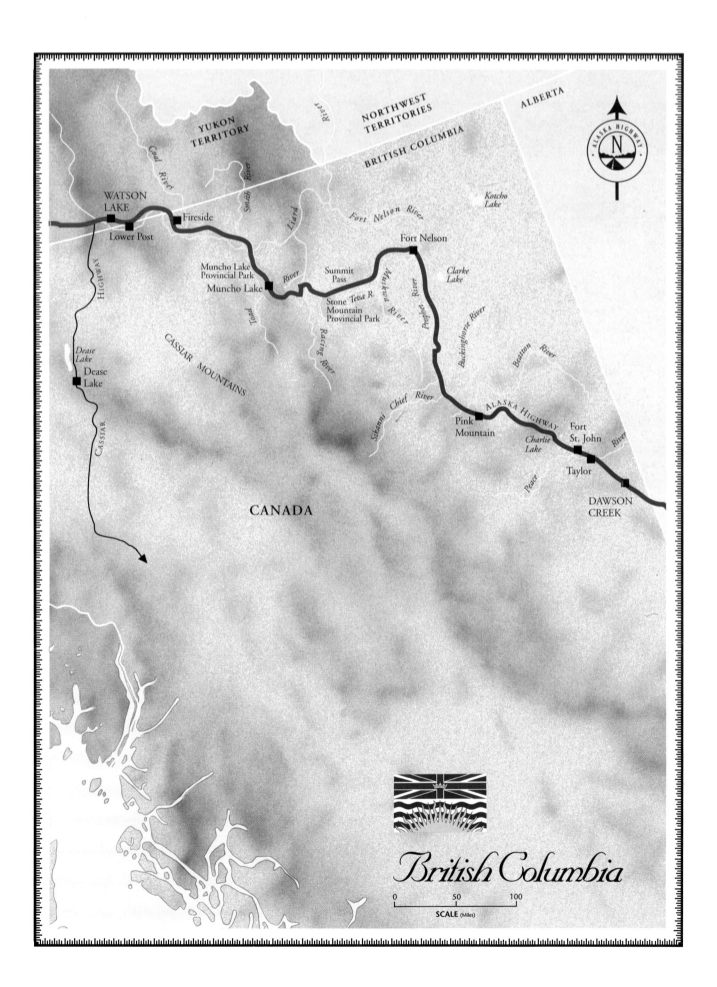

British Columbia

DAWSON CREEK
TO PINK MOUNTAIN

Dawson Creek, British Columbia, is where the adventure begins. Nestled at the edge of Peace River country in the province's northeast corner, this agricultural community is blanketed with bright yellow and green expanses of grain. Each summer, this town of 12,000 comes alive as the first flurry of highway travelers begins its journey north.

The hub of four major thoroughfares, Dawson Creek has the distinction of being Mile 0 on the Alaska Highway. Milepost designations were first put up to help motorists and workers orient themselves in the wilderness. It wasn't long before places along the highway's route were referred to in terms of how far they were from the starting point, Dawson Creek. Now the custom is more nostalgic than informative: because the highway is continually improved and straightened, milepost distances indicated are no longer accurate, and travelers will notice many discrepancies between their odometers and the signposts.

Most of the first mileposts have disappeared from the roadside, but they haven't vanished entirely from the culture of the highway. They are still used in mailing addresses and as reference points. The original Alaska Highway cairn is preserved in the Northern Alberta Railway Park in Dawson Creek, and each July the community celebrates its relationship to the highway with Mile 0 Days.

LEFT: THE ORIGINAL ALASKA HIGHWAY CAIRN IS PRESERVED IN THE NORTHERN ALBERTA RAILWAY PARK, IN DAWSON CREEK, WHERE TRAVELERS CAN ALSO EXPLORE A VISITORS' CENTER AND ART GALLERY.
RIGHT: MILEPOST 0 BRIGHTENS A DOWNTOWN INTERSECTION IN DAWSON CREEK, WHERE THE ALASKA HIGHWAY OFFICIALLY BEGINS

Dawson Creek's namesake was Canadian surveyor and geologist George Mercer Dawson, who led expeditions through the area in the late 1880s. His painstaking reports laid the groundwork for further exploration. Partly as a result of Dawson's accounts of the valley's fertile soil, homesteaders flocked to this part of the province around the turn of the century. Because of their success, farming now is an important part of the area's economy. Grain crops, grass seed, and the raising of animals contribute to a gross income of over $30 million annually. An especially popular enterprise is canola—the Cinderella crop of the prairies. This bright yellow flowering plant is a member of the mustard family. When pressed, the seeds yield oil low in acid and cholesterol, excellent for cooking and as a base for margarine. Much of the raw seed is exported to Japan.

Canola isn't the only international export from this small community. One entrepreneur gave up his cattle operations to raise bison. The exotic meat ironically is not available to local residents: the rancher exports his product to Europe. Bison herds are found both in the wild and in captivity at several points along the highway.

This can be dangerous to animals and humans, because it emboldens the bear, causing it to lose its natural inhibitions about contact.

It's now known that bears, once thought to suffer poor eyesight, have vision similar to humans'. They also have highly developed abilities to smell and hear. Bears are good swimmers, and can run up to 40 miles an hour over a short distance.

As we look into the future, bears have more to fear from humans. The species is notoriously sensitive to the disturbance of its habitat. Factors such as the construction of pipelines and general encroachment of civilization are likely to lessen the habitat and winter den environment available to the animal, in turn decreasing the number of bears that can survive.

Highway travelers will find plenty of opportunities to observe these impressive creatures. Bears are most often spotted from the road in the early morning or in the evening.

BLACK BEARS ARE COMMON SIGHTS
ALL ALONG THE ALASKA HIGHWAY.

It's called bearanoia. The first days along the Alaska Highway, even the most stalwart traveler is convinced there's something hiding in the bushes. One cause may be an avalanche of crazed-bear stories, like the one about the grizzly who attacked the campers in a national park and . . .

Despite the scary tales, bear attacks are rare, and most frequently involve mother bears with cubs. Bear encounters, on the other hand, are common. That makes sense; grizzlies and black bears are numerous in Canada and Alaska. But bears prefer to avoid people. Making plenty of noise is one way to give bears fair warning to flee. Hikers should also exercise common sense, not venturing into terrain clearly marked by bear trails.

While their preferred diet is vegetation, bears are omnivorous opportunists. Leaving food out is a way to unwittingly attract the animal's attention.

The Peace River valley has yielded other opportunities besides farming. In recent years, rich deposits of natural gas and petroleum were discovered, transforming the town of Taylor into a major industrial center. Along with a large sawmill, a natural gas processing plant and several oil refineries dominate the tiny community (population 900). Taylor also marks the beginning of a 700-mile-long natural gas pipeline serving Vancouver and western Washington State.

Beyond the rich Taylor Flats area is the historic settlement of Fort St. John. First established in 1806, Fort St. John's original site was on the Peace River, about 10 miles south. It served as a fur-trading post for the Sikanni and Beaver Indians, the first inhabitants of the Peace River region. (Despite its name, the river is thought to have once served as a boundary between warring Indian tribes.)

Enticed by the land's bounty, fur traders first appeared in the Fort St. John region in the late eighteenth century. They hunted the plentiful mink, marten, beaver, fox, wolf, muskrat, fisher, and wolverine. These trappers, along with prospectors and the local

Natives, would remain the community's primary residents until well into the twentieth century. In the 1950s, a new resource would lure outsiders. Oil derricks sprouted around the community, giving Fort St. John a nickname: Land of New Totems.

Surrounding Fort St. John is a lush countryside threaded by lakes and streams. At 10-mile-long Charlie Lake, two provincial parks provide opportunities to play golf, swim, fish, and go boating. Despite the appearance of civilization in this area, it lies at the edge of wilderness. Unsuspecting motorists are often surprised to catch sight of a shy deer—or a family of coyotes—by the side of the road.

LEFT: BOATERS ON TRANQUIL CHARLIE LAKE, LOCATED JUST OUTSIDE FORT ST. JOHN, TEST THEIR LINES. WALLEYE ARE PLENTIFUL HERE.

ABOVE: HIGHWAY TRAVELERS CATCH THEIR FIRST GLIMPSE OF BISON NEAR DAWSON CREEK.

PINK MOUNTAIN
TO SUMMIT PASS

LEFT: FEW OF THE HARDY MOTORISTS WHO TACKLED THE ALASKA HIGHWAY IN THE 1940S WOULD RECOGNIZE THIS SMOOTH STRETCH NEAR PROPHET RIVER.
RIGHT: LONG-TIME AREA RESIDENT MARL BROWN SPEARHEADED CREATION OF THE FORT NELSON HERITAGE MUSEUM, A TESTAMENT TO THE COMMUNITY'S PAST.

ink Mountain is named for the color of its sandstone composition. Because sandstone is more resistant to erosion than the shale of the surrounding region, area elevations gradually rise; the community of Pink Mountain is 3,600 feet above sea level. For the next 50 miles heading northwest, mountains and hills are mesalike in appearance. Over eons, numerous rivers have shaped them, carving deep incisions.

Traversing the Rocky Mountain foothills, the road crosses the Beatton, Sikanni Chief, and Buckinghorse rivers, where anglers find pike, grayling, and whitefish. Then it makes a gradual descent back to the valley floor. Ahead, a new bypass has shaved miles from the road. Completed in 1987, the section offers an alternative to the original route to the summit of Trutch Mountain, which is steep and treacherous.

Situated at the confluence of the Prophet, Muskwa, and Sikanni Chief rivers, Fort Nelson also originated as a fur-trading post in the early 1800s. The region was first inhabited by the Slavey Indians, an Athapaskan people who migrated from the Great Slave Lake in the Northwest Territories. Many Natives still live in the area. Fort Nelson's setting vividly recalls the time when waterways, not highways, were the lifeblood of transportation for the region. As late as the 1930s, Fort Nelson still depended on riverboats to deliver supplies, and sled dogs and pack horses were the

mainstay of overland travel.

Fur trapping is still practiced in the area, but on a much smaller scale. Technology has dramatically changed the trapper's lifestyle. Dogsleds have given way to snowmobiles, and the task of setting a trapline no longer means arduously cutting a swath through the wilderness. Now trappers can follow the existing trails and paths of fuel pipelines through the forests. Traplines are set on government lands, and trappers must first obtain licenses. These can be bought and sold, and are continually changing hands. About 100 families in the area make their living trapping. Full-time practitioners can earn as much as $50,000 a year.

Just outside Fort Nelson, the road crosses the Muskwa River bridge—at 1,000 feet above sea level, it represents the lowest point on the highway. Mountain streams to the west drain into the river,

OUTSIDE FORT NELSON, THE MUSKWA RIVER DESCENDS TO 1,000 FEET ABOVE SEA LEVEL, THE LOWEST POINT ON THE HIGHWAY.

the course of establishing its far-flung empire, the company became enormously powerful. In 1868, the British Parliament forced the company to turn over its vast territorial holdings to Canada. The firm's business enterprises, however, continue to the present day. They extend across the breadth of Canada, from urban department stores—called The Bay—to rural outposts.

ABOVE: A HUDSON'S BAY COMPANY CACHE, 1921.
BELOW: ROBERT CAMPBELL OF THE HUDSON'S BAY COMPANY IN THE MID-1800S.

The furs of the Pacific Northwest captivated the world long before the region's first gold rush. The Russian traders established a lucrative headquarters in Sitka, Alaska, in the early 1800s, and gradually expanded inland throughout Canada and south to California. By the middle of the century, Russian interests were replaced by a new power—the Hudson's Bay Company.

The Hudson's Bay Company was founded in the 1600s in London as a trading firm. When the vast economic potential of the North American fur trade became apparent, the company pursued this industry with ferocity, and in 1670 it received a historic charter from the king of England. Charles II gave the company title to all lands draining into northern Canada's Hudson Bay—over 1,400,000 square miles. The company further enlarged the area under its control by hiring canny, tough employees, zealous men such as Robert Campbell.

A Scotsman and inveterate explorer, Campbell is thought to be the first European to enter the interior of the Yukon, in 1840. Known for his sensitivity in dealings with Natives, Campbell carefully recorded the landforms and wildlife encountered in his travels throughout British Columbia and the Yukon Territory. These accounts proved immensely valuable in subsequent expeditions by explorers and scientists.

Eventually Hudson's Bay trading posts extended from the Arctic to California. In

THE CRYSTAL-CLEAR TETSA RIVER BECKONS FISHERMEN TO WATERS BRIMMING WITH DOLLY VARDEN, ARCTIC GRAYLING, AND WHITEFISH.

causing frequent flooding each spring. The road weaves its way through the last 50 miles of Canada's Interior Plains before beginning a gradual ascent. It passes a series of landforms with names that are conscientiously descriptive: flat-topped Table Mountain, pointed Tepee Mountain, profile-shaped Indian Head Rock, and precipitous Teetering Rock.

The highway parallels the Tetsa River for 20 miles, offering frustrated fly fishermen the chance to test their lines in uncrowded waters. Fossil hunters and rockhounds may also make discoveries here. Tetsa's riverbed contains coral fossils along with quartzite pebbles and rocks patterned in a succession of tones: red to maroon, and white to cream. The stones are fine-grained and take a good polish.

The Tetsa River area is also famed for its big-game hunting. These lands are managed by the government to ensure protection of the wildlife populations. Hunts are costly, some running $1,000 per day, per person. Today, many big-game hunting operations try to diversify their businesses with backcountry trips for a new breed of shooters—photographers.

Climbing through the Front Range of the Rocky Mountains, the Alaska Highway reaches its highest point at Summit Pass—4,250 feet. Peaks in the vicinity top 7,000 feet. The Stone Mountain Range offers hikes to alpine lakes accented by wildflowers and waterfalls. A special attraction is the haunting forest of hoodoos—unusual formations of hard-rock cores caused by erosion. This high country is also an excellent place to view wildlife. Mountain goats, Stone sheep, caribou, and bear are year-round residents.

LEFT: A LONE CARIBOU SAUNTERS ALONG THE ROADSIDE IN EARLY SUMMER. THE SOLITARY JOURNEY IS UNUSUAL; THESE ANIMALS MORE FREQUENTLY TRAVEL IN HERDS. *ABOVE:* STONE MOUNTAIN PROVINCIAL PARK COMES ALIVE IN MID-SEPTEMBER, ITS LANDSCAPE A SPLASH OF BRILLIANT HUES.

SUMMIT PASS TO
YUKON BORDER

*I*n Stone Mountain Provincial Park, the weather changes
in a heartbeat. Because of the park's elevation and
northern latitude, snow is possible any time of the year.
Storms can blow through quickly, catching travelers
unprepared. One minute, temperatures are climbing;
the next, cloud cover sends them plummeting.

The changeable weather matches the landscape's
diversity. Carved and molded by glaciers during the last
ice age, lower mountain slopes are covered by glacial
till, a composition of clay, sand, gravel, and boulders.
Mountains in this area were formed by the gentle
faulting of sediments. A formation such as Folded
Mountain seems to have surrealistic dimensions as the
sunlight casts shadows on the crevices of its face.

From Summit Pass, the road descends through a
dramatic gorge cut in the earth's rock. The canyon
separates the Tetsa River system from the MacDonald
River system. For the next stretch, the road hugs
MacDonald Creek, bypassing numerous gullies and
waterfalls. Several small hot springs surprise the
traveler just north of the highway, where the Racing
River meets the Toad. The latter river was named by
highway workers, who discovered numerous small
toads nearby. The hot springs provided workers with
a respite from the toil of the highway.

Following the buff-colored gorge of the Toad River,
the road dips into a valley shaped by the waters of the

*LEFT: EAST OF SUMMIT PASS,
THE ALASKA HIGHWAY CUTS
A WIDE SHELF ALONG A ROCKY
MOUNTAINSIDE.*
*RIGHT: ENCOUNTERS WITH
WILDLIFE SUCH AS THIS
WHITE-TAILED DEER ARE
AMONG THE MANY PLEASURES
OF HIGHWAY TRAVEL.*

river. What follows is one of British Columbia's brightest jewels—emerald green Muncho Lake. Muncho is a Slavey Indian word for "deep lake." Just how far down the waters go isn't known, although depths exceeding 500 feet have been estimated. The lake is ice-covered for five months of the year. Even in the summer its temperature averages only 42 degrees Fahrenheit.

The lake is flanked by the steep, forested slopes of the Rocky Mountain Terminal Range on the west and the rock-faced Sentinel Range on the east. The Terminal Range is rich in iron-based minerals, which give its sharp exposures their rusty hues. Shot with copper, the Sentinels leach copper oxide into the lake, producing its incredible blue-green color. Several mammoth washes sweep dramatically down to the shores of the lake. During heavy rains, the caverns of hidden underground rivers overflow and the washes run for two or three hours. Treasures have been forced to the surface during this ancient process, including a variety of aquatic fossils such as prehistoric clams and corals.

ABOVE: "YOU HAVE TO BE A BIT HARD-NOSED TO MAKE IT," SAYS MUNCHO LAKE RESIDENT JACK GUNNESS. ONE OF A HANDFUL OF INDIVIDUALS WHO LIVE YEAR-ROUND AT THE LAKE, GUNNESS AND HIS FAMILY OPERATE A TOUR-GUIDE BUSINESS.
RIGHT: FISHING, WILDLIFE VIEWING, AND ROCKHOUNDING ARE AMONG THE PURSUITS AWAITING MUNCHO LAKE VISITORS.

STONE SHEEP

A SHEDDING STONE SHEEP PAUSES TO STUDY TRAVELERS
NEAR MUNCHO LAKE.

Columbia and the southeastern corner of the Yukon, Stone sheep are called "thinhorns." Their horns spread and spiral more than the bighorns', and tips point away from the face. A female's horns are backswept and short. A male's make a spiral that can measure more than three feet in length. The age of a sheep is determined by the number of growth rings in its horns. There is a strict social hierarchy among the animals, and the ram with the largest horns dominates the group.

Due to their migratory patterns, Stone sheep are generally seen in late spring and early summer, and reside in alpine meadows throughout the summer.

One of the most endearing creatures found in the North is the Stone sheep. Meandering near the roadside or feeding at a mineral lick, the sheep will often stop to scrutinize passersby. Large, protruding eyes give them a curious look, while spiraling horns add a contrasting flare of dignity.

Stone sheep are distant relatives of Rocky Mountain bighorn sheep and of the same species as Dall. Unlike the snowy white Dall, the Stone's color varies, from gray to brown or black, with a white muzzle, belly, and rump patch.

Different colors occur within the same species as a result of adaptation. During the last glacial period, the sheep population in the region was split, leaving it in two habitats. The Dall lived on alpine slopes close to glaciers, the Stone in treed, mountainous areas. Two colorations evolved.

Found only in northern British

Muncho Lake Provincial Park and several private campgrounds give travelers a moment to catch their breath. Lingcod, whitefish, and lake trout are commonly caught in Muncho Lake. The lake is stocked with 10,000 rainbow trout each spring. When the ice first breaks in the spring, it is possible to catch a lake trout averaging 40 to 50 pounds. In this habitat, fish grow slowly—perhaps one-half pound per year. At that rate, the age of a 50-pound trout is estimated to be 100 years. Local residents respect these old-timers, taking care not to overfish the lake. A variety of wildlife can be observed in the park, including Stone sheep and the rare woodland caribou. At the mineral lick north of Muncho Lake, mountain sheep supplement their diet with minerals found in the soil.

Leaving the northern Canadian Rockies, the highway meets the mighty Liard River, forming the mountains' northern boundary. The French originally named it *Riviere aux Liards*, meaning river of cottonwood trees. Just outside Liard River Hot Springs, a picturesque suspension bridge spans the river. The only suspension bridge on the Alaska Highway, it was constructed using some salvage from "Galloping Gertie," the old Tacoma Narrows Bridge that collapsed in Washington in a windstorm in November 1940.

Now a provincial park, the springs offer visitors a soothing soak in mineral water, with temperatures exceeding 120 degrees Fahrenheit. Encouraged by the humid air, unusual flora and fauna thrive here. Moss grows on terraces around the park's pool, creating mysterious hanging gardens and an air of intrigue. The microclimate results in an interesting phenomenon: many plants and small animals not usually found in the North can survive here.

The highway follows the Liard River into the Yukon Territory, traversing the Liard Plain. Smith River marks the eastern boundary of the Liard Plain, a region of rolling plateaus with low, rounded hills and deep valleys. Now the landscape's geological makeup is dramatically revealed. At Smith River Falls, water crashes down canyon walls of black shale, spraying fishermen at its base with a light mist. Coal River flows through a large deposit of coal, visible in the riverbed and beside its banks. During the highway's construction, workers used the coal for fuel. The swirling waters of Whirlpool Canyon are formed as water rushes over tilted shale. The constant pressure polishes the deposits. When the river recedes in the late summer, the rocks glisten as the sun's rays bounce off microquartz crystals.

Not all the forces of nature evident along the road are so beautiful. The traveler meets the harsher side when passing the

LEFT: FATIGUED HIGHWAY DRIVERS REPLENISH THEIR SPIRIT OF ADVENTURE WITH A SOAK IN THE MINERAL-RICH WATERS AT LIARD RIVER HOT SPRINGS PROVINCIAL PARK.

TOP: NEW GROWTH EMERGES AT THE SITE OF THE EG FIRE, ONE OF THE LARGEST IN BRITISH COLUMBIA'S HISTORY.

BOTTOM: THIS LOWER POST CITIZEN DISPLAYS A COLLECTION EMINENTLY SUITED TO HIS ROADSIDE RESIDENCE: HUBCAPS.

barren, eerie land near Fireside. The 1982 Eg fire was the second largest in British Columbia's history, burning more than 400,000 acres. Beyond the apparent destruction, forest fires burn off excess underbrush and open the forest floor to sunlight, allowing new vegetation to sprout. The fresh growth in turn attracts and supports more wildlife. In the environs of the Eg fire, deer are returning for the first time in years.

Allen's Lookout provides sweeping views of the Liard River, which was a major transportation route at the turn of the century. Once riverboats filled the Liard, their holds brimming with furs and

supplies. Another brush with history occurs at nearby Contact Creek bridge. Here, in September of 1942, Alaska Highway construction crews working west from Fort Nelson and those struggling east from Whitehorse met.

Following the Liard River, the road snakes back and forth three times across the Yukon border before making a final commitment. Lower Post is the last community it passes in British Columbia. First established as a Hudson's Bay Company trading post near the mouth of the Dease River, it is now a Native settlement.

TURBULENT WATERS
MESMERIZE ONLOOKERS AT
WHIRLPOOL CANYON.

Contrasts mark the majestic Yukon Territory, a place of extremes in temperature and terrain. Winters are long and harsh, but they give way to springs and summers of unusual intensity. The Yukon has experienced the lowest recorded temperature in Canada—minus 81 degrees Fahrenheit. Yet during the summer months, when sunlight may linger for 20 hours or more, the mercury can soar to above 90.

Crystal-clear waterways, jagged peaks, and wide, rolling valleys are commonplace in this immense land. While competition for the traveler's attention is intense, two territorial trophies nevertheless stand out: 19,850-foot Mount Logan, Canada's highest peak, and the mighty Yukon River. The country's longest and largest waterway, the Yukon River flows 2,000 miles before it empties into the Bering Sea.

Landlocked by British Columbia to the south, the Yukon Territory is bounded by Alaska on the west and the Northwest Territories to the east. At its narrowest point, it touches the Beaufort Sea. The territory's 186,000 square miles are inhabited by fewer than 30,000 people, resulting in one of the most sparsely populated regions on earth.

The Yukon is filled with a dense wildlife community. Moose, black bears, grizzlies, caribou, eagles, Dall sheep, and bison are among the animals highway motorists are likely to meet. Explorers of

LEFT: OUTSIDE OF KLUANE LAKE IN THE YUKON TERRITORY, THE ROAD RISES TO MEET THE MOUNTAINS IN WINTER. *ABOVE:* A TESLIN-AREA TLINGIT GIRL, AROUND 1930.

Overleaf: The season's first snowfall blankets the awesome Dawson Range, south of Beaver Creek.

Above: One-half century ago, Ed Karmen ventured north to work on the highway. Today, he and his wife, Betty, make their home just a few hundred yards from the road he helped construct.

backcountry treasures such as Kluane National Park will encounter many more species.

Those who journey along the Alaska Highway through the Yukon will spend almost 600 miles in this pristine wilderness, leaving congested cities behind. Dazzled by the breathtaking terrain, some may be tempted to cover as much ground as possible, forgoing stops at intriguing cafes and other points of interest. But each tiny settlement possesses a unique voice and history. The visitor may recall an afternoon huddled in conversation with a Yukoner as vividly as memories of a magnificent mountain.

While today's Yukon Territory seems a place apart, at one time "Yukon" was a household word. Shouts rang out around the world in 1896 when George Carmack, Skookum Jim Mason, and Charlie Tagish found gold in Bonanza Creek near Dawson City. It was the start of the Klondike gold rush, and for the next several years, frenzied stampeders flooded the territory. Numbering as many as 60,000, they came from all over the world. Western merchants of all stripes—from cities such as Seattle and San Francisco to the smallest hamlets of Canada—profited by outfitting the gold seeker. It was the prospector who didn't necessarily prosper. Most would depart without wealth, but their presence forever changed the Yukon. They opened up settlement in this isolated land, helping to smooth the path for those who followed.

European residents prior to the gold rush were few, an assortment of independent prospectors, trappers, and explorers. They were preceded by the Natives, believed to have made the Yukon their home as early as 30,000 years ago. In time, the Tlingit and Athapaskan people settled along the Yukon Basin, a vast area extending deep into Alaska. The seminomadic Athapaskans especially flourished in the river environment. Their seasonal migrations took them across the breadth of Alaska and Canada, and along the Pacific Northwest coast. Regardless of group, the Natives shared a reliance on the land. The connection shaped relationships, religious beliefs, settlement patterns, and dress. Fascinating distinctions also existed, even among close neighbors. But intermarriage, trade, and warfare eventually blurred many of the boundaries of their rich cultures and varied languages.

Today, 20 percent of the territory's population—over 5,000 individuals—claim some Native heritage. Dotting the highway, museums and interpretative centers trace the history and traditions of these indigenous peoples. Some Natives maintain the hunting and fishing lifestyles of their ancestors, although they have discovered

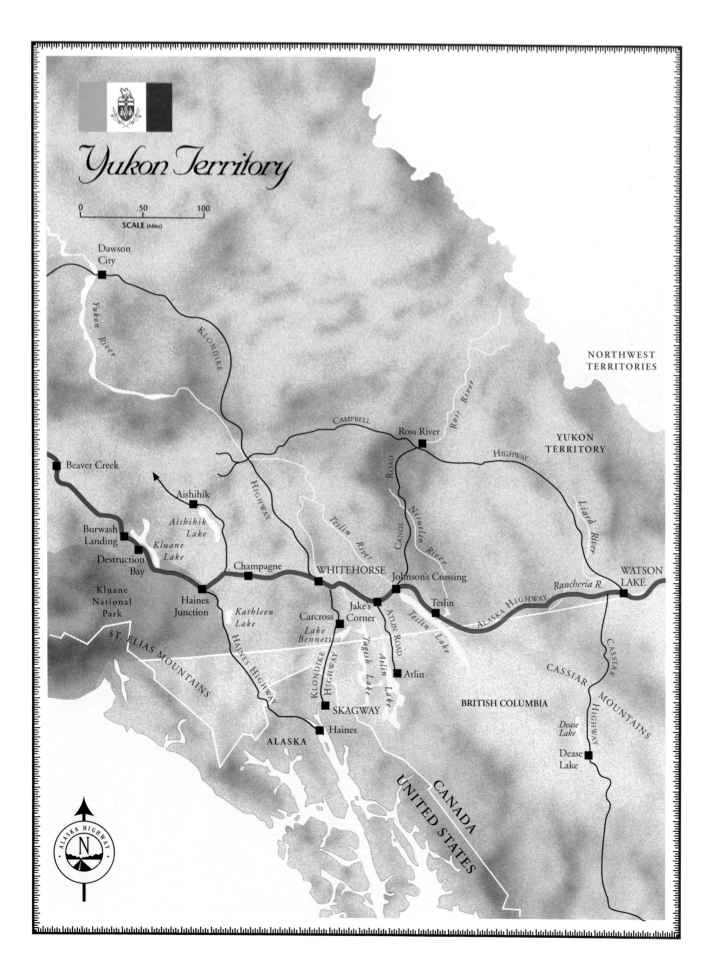

Yukon Territory

SCALE (Miles)
0   50   100

Dawson City

Yukon River

KLONDIKE

CAMPBELL

Ross River

Ross River

NORTHWEST TERRITORIES

YUKON TERRITORY

Beaver Creek

Aishihik

ROAD

HIGHWAY

Liard River

Aishihik Lake

Burwash Landing

Kluane Lake

Teslin River

CANOL

Nisutlin River

HIGHWAY

Destruction Bay

Champagne

WHITEHORSE

Johnson's Crossing

Rancheria R.

WATSON LAKE

Kluane National Park

Haines Junction

Kathleen Lake

Carcross

Jake's Corner

Teslin

Alaska Highway

Lake Bennett

Teslin Lake

ST. ELIAS MOUNTAINS

HAINES HIGHWAY

KLONDIKE HIGHWAY

Tagish Lake

ATLIN ROAD

Atlin Lake

Atlin

CASSIAR MOUNTAINS

CASSIAR HIGHWAY

BRITISH COLUMBIA

SKAGWAY

Haines

Dease Lake

ALASKA

Dease Lake

CANADA

UNITED STATES

ALASKA HIGHWAY
N

ways to adapt these ancient endeavors to modern purposes. They operate numerous fishing and hunting guide services, and offer their elegant handicrafts and artwork for sale.

Despite the territory's few inhabitants, visitors here will not lack for services and local expertise. Tourism is second only to mining among the Yukon's industries. Gregarious Yukoners have opened their homes to travelers since gold rush days. Many of the restaurants, bakeries, and motels built to serve highway workers in the 1940s are still in business today.

Before the existence of the Alaska Highway, would-be adventurers could dream about the journey north, but only the hardiest dared make the trip. Creation of the road opened the wonders of the Yukon to everyone.

LEFT: A CANOEIST PADDLES DOWN THE CLEAR TESLIN RIVER, FAVORED FOR ITS EXPANSES OF PLACID WATERS.

ABOVE: A YOUNG ELK PRANCES THROUGH THE SNOW IN THE YUKON WILDLIFE PRESERVE NEAR WHITEHORSE.

YUKON BORDER TO
JOHNSON'S CROSSING

atson Lake is just north of the border of British
Columbia, in the southeast portion of the Yukon
Territory. As a sign posted near its entrance proclaims,
this town is the official "Gateway to the Yukon." First
settled as a trading post, the community is believed to
have been named for a British gold prospector, Frank
Watson. Just as it did in the early 1900s, the town
continues to provide services to hunters, trappers, and
fishermen. But over time, this community of 1,600 has
evolved into a major transportation center with a
busy airport. Located on both the Alaska and Campbell
highways, Watson Lake is also close to the Cassiar
Highway turnoff.

Fittingly, the town's major tourist attraction—the
Signpost Forest—has to do with travel. Finding himself
far from home as part of the road-building effort, a G.I.
started the "forest" in 1942. It consists of road signs,
license plates, and other highway memorabilia. Over
the decades, thousands of obliging tourists have added
their own contributions. Just behind the forest is a
visitors' center, offering an interpretative display about
the Alaska Highway.

Neighboring Watson Lake Recreation Park offers
opportunities for camping, swimming, and picnicking.
The lake is host to trout and northern pike, but
anglers may want to consider a more exotic fishing
experience. Local air taxi services can arrange fly-in

LEFT: TRAVELERS FROM AROUND
THE WORLD LEAVE SOUVENIRS OF
HOME BEHIND AT THE SIGNPOST
FOREST IN WATSON LAKE.
RIGHT: INTRICATE BURL CARVING
IS A PRIZED ART FORM IN THE
YUKON.

jaunts to remote lakes in the bush. Here the catch is likely to be extraordinary. Even if no 38-pound trophy is forthcoming, tourists will gain unforgettable glimpses from the air of the backcountry landscape.

Outside of Watson Lake, the road heads due west, crossing the upper reaches of the Liard River. The discovery of gold created a mini-rush here in 1872. Some of the precious metal is still embedded in the river's sandbars, awaiting the next generation of stampeders. Those interested in trying their luck at panning may do so, but they're advised to first check with the local mining and records office. Many gold mines—and claims—are still in operation.

After the Cassiar Highway junction, the Alaska Highway continues across the Liard Plain, reaching elevations of 2,000 to 3,000 feet. For the next 100 miles of landscape, rivers carve their

CRYSTALLINE RIVERS LIKE THE RANCHERIA PASS WITHIN A WHISPER OF THE HIGHWAY.

promising river has been worked and every rock turned in search of gold.

The process of finding and extracting the precious metal has also grown extremely sophisticated. Contemporary gold operations are usually commercial, requiring a large capital investment and several employees. Bulldozers, front-end loaders, motor-driven pumps, and conveyor belts have replaced the hand-hewn sluice boxes of early prospectors.

While placer mining continues to produce significant amounts of gold, hard-rock or lode mining promises to yield even greater quantities. Traditional placer mining sifts through loose, light materials like gravel, sand, or mud, leaving behind the heavier gold. Hard-rock mining recovers minerals from hard-rock deposits. In the past, emphasis was on placer mining, leaving hard-rock mining as a viable alternative.

Despite the technology involved in serious gold mining, highway travelers armed with a pan and a shovel can still experience the excitement of discovering gold. Recreational gold panning in many Yukon rivers and streams is likely to net at least a few flecks of the elusive metal.

THE CALL OF GOLD STILL DRAWS FORTUNE SEEKERS TO THE YUKON, JUST AS IT DID IN THE NINETEENTH CENTURY.

Each year hundreds of letters deluge a small government office in the town of Whitehorse. "We are interested in relocating to the Yukon," one hopeful writes. "Can you give me any information on how people get claims? What are the rules for dredging?" Nearly a century after the fabled Klondike gold rush, the myth persists that fortunes are here for the taking. While gold is still discovered in the Yukon, it's rare that an individual strikes it rich or even makes a living prospecting.

Part of the reason is the number of existing claims. Little of the territory remains unexamined or unstaked. According to many authorities, every

TOP: ANGLERS SEEK OUT THE TESLIN RIVER
FOR ITS EXCELLENT GRAYLING FISHING.
ABOVE: WIND RIPPLES THROUGH SQUIRREL GRASS.

courses through forests, leaving paths of winding valleys. Here, the highway crosses the Continental Divide, and the water flow changes. The Rancheria River flows eastward, joining the MacKenzie River system. Westward-flowing rivers, like the Swift and the Morley, drain into the Pacific via the Yukon River system. From this point, all rivers and streams crossed on the highway drain into the Pacific watershed. Prized grayling swim in the unpolluted waters of Little Rancheria Creek, and the Swift, Rancheria, and Morley rivers.

Inanimate treasures also abound. A semiprecious stone deposit near Seagull Creek is yet another reminder of the rich nature of this land. In 1960, this deposit of topaz, fluorite, and tourmaline was found on the north face of a nearby mountain. Specimens have been placed in museums around the world.

To the south, the Cassiar Mountains provide a dramatic backdrop. Triangular Simpson Peak juts 7,130 feet into the air, the highest point in the northern part of the range. For the next 40 miles the highway traverses the Yukon plateau, an area of deep valleys punctuated by gently rounded hills.

The community of Teslin is located at the meeting of Nisutlin River and Teslin Lake, one of three major lakes in the area. (The others are Atlin and Tagish.) Derived from the Tlingit language, Teslin means "long, narrow water." Before reaching the village, the road goes over the Nisutlin Bay bridge; at a length of nearly 2,000 feet, it is the longest water span on the highway.

With a population of 450, Teslin possesses one of the largest concentrations of Natives in the Yukon, many of whom practice a traditional subsistence lifestyle. Most are interior, or inland, Tlingit. The Tlingit are a Pacific Northwest Coast Indian group residing primarily in Southeast Alaska, although some have settled inland. Visitors who want to learn more about Tlingit culture will find an opportunity in the George Johnston Museum. A Tlingit, Johnston was also an accomplished photographer. His subjects were the Natives of Teslin and the nearby British Columbia community of Atlin in the first half of the century, and many of these striking photos are on view here.

Departing Teslin, the highway makes its way between Teslin Lake to the west and the Big Salmon Range of the Pelly Mountain system to the east. Here the road crosses numerous creeks with evocative names: Tenmile, Lone Tree, Deadman's. Not all the designations are of mysterious origin. Deadman's Hill—from which the creek drains—resembles a reclining man. Many names are the plainspoken legacy of prospectors. Miners often substituted their personal choices for place names, and sometimes the new nomenclature stuck.

Just short of the Teslin River bridge, which boasts another formidable water span, the route intersects with the Canol Road. Originally called the Canadian Oil Road, this thoroughfare was also the result of a World War II project. Along with their plans for the Alaska Highway and the Northwest Staging Route, military officials envisioned an oil pipeline from the Northwest Territories to a refinery in Whitehorse. The result was a 500-mile gravel road, a pipeline, and a refinery. All were abandoned in 1945.

Today, 139 miles of the south Canol Road are maintained to Ross River, where the road meets the Campbell Highway. The north section of the Canol Road leads northeast from Ross River and dead-ends in the Northwest Territories.

Across the Teslin River bridge is Johnson's Crossing: a gas station, small store, restaurant, and several camping sites. During the building of the bridge and the Canol Road, it was the site of a U.S. Army Corps of Engineers camp.

TOP: TLINGIT PHOTOGRAPHER GEORGE JOHNSTON WAS FAMED FOR IMAGES LIKE THIS ONE OF A YOUNG TESLIN BOY.

ABOVE: WATSON SMARCH, A TLINGLIT, HELPED HIGHWAY SURVEYORS MARK THE TRAIL IN THE 1940S. TODAY HE OPERATES A FISHING AND HUNTING GUIDE SERVICE IN TESLIN.

JOHNSON'S CROSSING
TO HAINES JUNCTION

For the 1890s prospector, treacherous travel was tempered by the promise of gold in the Klondike. Having made the long voyage up the Pacific Coast by steamship, some traveled the Stikine River to Telegraph Creek, then journeyed overland to Teslin Lake. At the lake, they constructed rafts and small boats and floated the Teslin and Yukon rivers the rest of the way to Dawson City. Amazingly, the majority survived the difficult passage. Impetuousness cost the lives of many others.

Today, this route remains a favored one in this part of the Yukon, but for a different kind of prospecting. Johnson's Crossing is a popular jumping-off spot for canoe trips to Dawson City via the Teslin and Yukon rivers. During the trip, which usually takes around two weeks, visitors search for wildlife rather than gold. The area is rich in muskrat, eagles, moose, and wolves.

Those electing to drive will find the road turns west. At Jake's Corner, the traveler has a choice of two appealing side trips. One is a scenic 60-mile southern route terminating in Atlin, British Columbia, a Native village situated on Atlin Lake. The alternative heads west for 33 miles and ends in Carcross on Bennett Lake. Named for the large herds of caribou that once crossed on their annual migrations, Carcross is the site of one of the region's oldest continuously operated inns, the Caribou Hotel.

LEFT: NOW IN DRYDOCK, THE SS *KLONDIKE* RECALLS THE GLORIOUS DAYS WHEN THE STERN-WHEELER RULED THE YUKON.

RIGHT: WILD ROSEBUSHES ORNAMENT THE HIGHWAY IN JULY.

Atlin partisans make no small claims. To them, the community is merely "the Switzerland of North America." Perched above the longest (90 miles) natural lake in the province and surrounded by mountains, it is spectacularly beautiful. The Lewellyn Glacier, hillsides of alpine flowers, and a retired stern-wheeler, the MV *Tarahne,* are among the attractions. For those willing to be waylaid longer than an afternoon, the community sponsors an artists' summer school.

Visitors to Carcross may want to continue south to Skagway, Alaska, a 66-mile journey on Klondike Highway 2. Reached through razor-sharp turns along dramatic slopes, Skagway marks the trailhead for the infamous Chilkoot Trail. Many selected difficult Chilkoot Pass as a route to the goldfields. Even today, the trail's challenges, culminating at the steep pass, inspire respect. When standing below the pass, hikers are awed as they look up the precipitous rocky incline and contemplate the gritty determination of those early pioneers. Skagway, a colorful town with many remnants of the gold rush days, is also a frequent stop for ferries and cruise ships sailing the Inside Passage.

Klondike Highway 2 returns to the Alaska Highway southeast of Whitehorse, the capital of the Yukon. Nestled in the elbow of the Yukon River and surrounded by limestone cliffs, Whitehorse is home to two-thirds of the territory's population, around 20,000 residents. Located in a four-mile-wide valley, the town is believed to have taken its name from the early prospectors' vision of the foaming rapids outside of Miles Canyon. The miners believed it resembled the mane of a white horse.

Miles Canyon is located just inside the Whitehorse city limits. At the turn of the century, this narrow canyon with its vertical basalt walls and raging waters took the lives of many fortune seekers pressing on to the Klondike goldfields. Today, the former turbulence has been tamed by a hydroelectric power dam, and the rapids are no longer visible. Visitors can now explore the 3,000-foot-long, 90-foot-wide canyon through safe and pleasurable means. A footbridge spans the gorge, and day cruises are available on the river.

Whitehorse is the largest town on the Alaska Highway and its energy is infectious. On every corner the romance of the gold rush days is recalled. Old log cabins are sandwiched between new hotels and shops. Businesses emulate the bygone era with charming facades. Young men decked out in replicas of old North West Mounted Police uniforms patrol the streets, ready to assist tourists with information and directions.

MODERN-DAY RIVER RUNNERS TOUR MILES CANYON, ONCE THE SCOURGE OF THE GOLD SEEKER.

ELLEN DAVIGNON JOKES WITH VISITORS IN HER KITCHEN AT JOHNSON'S CROSSING.

It's 2:00 A.M. Ellen Davignon tiptoes out of her bedroom and begins the morning's routine at Johnson's Crossing Lodge. Within an hour, she is baking. In addition to her celebrated cinnamon rolls, Davignon makes a daily batch of white and whole-wheat bread. Next, 100 dainty butter tarts go in the oven, and an equal number of tiny meat pies. Apple and cherry tarts complete the day's line. By 9:00 A.M., Davignon has gone through 100 pounds of flour.

Davignon and the Alaska Highway grew up together. She moved to Johnson's Crossing as a child in 1948, when her father purchased an abandoned U.S. Army Corps of Engineers camp. It was not an auspicious start. The camp was without electricity or running water, and overnight customers had to settle for a Quonset hut. "We're not poor," she remembers her mother saying.

"We just don't have any money." Out of that hardscrabble beginning emerged a roadside institution of remarkable resourcefulness.

Over time, numerous amenities were added to the lodge, such as a cozy dining room and lobby. While it eventually acquired all the trappings of a proper inn, Davignon recalls that the lodge never served merely as a place to sleep and eat— that was too limited a role. It was also a gas station/tire shop, a movie theater, a politicians' hangout, a dance hall, and even, on occasion, a church.

Along with Johnson's Crossing Lodge, Davignon operates several other roadside businesses with her husband, Phil, and their five children. A columnist for the *Yukon News* in Whitehorse, she is also the author of *The Cinnamon Mine*, a delightful memoir of her childhood experiences.

THE MIGHTY YUKON—
CANADA'S LONGEST RIVER—HAS
BEEN WHITEHORSE'S LIFELINE FOR
NEARLY A CENTURY.

Because of its fortuitous placement near both the Yukon River and Skagway, Whitehorse grew quickly as a shipping and communications center. In 1900, the White Pass & Yukon Route railway was completed. Running between Skagway and Whitehorse, the train connected steamer travelers to Dawson City. (Portions of this famous old-time narrow gauge railroad still operate between Skagway and Whitehorse, offering a thrilling trip.) Over 250 sternwheelers crowded the river in those days, and one remains on display. The 210-foot SS *Klondike* was recently refurbished to its original glory.

The Yukon Gardens are another Whitehorse attraction, with a 20-acre botanical display. The gardens dispel any myth about the impossibility of flowers and plants thriving in the harsh North. Indigenous wild rosebushes, bright pink fireweed (Yukon's territorial flower), and several varieties of lupine are profuse in the gardens and can also be admired seasonally along the highway.

For rockhounds, a treasure trove of rare and unusual specimens can be found throughout the region. Over 45 types of minerals and rocks have been identified in the Whitehorse area. Local maps guide the way to deposits of elegant green malachite, steel gray hematite (the black diamond), colorful blue azurite, jasper, and many others. The Yukon Chamber of Mines in Whitehorse displays the various minerals and rocks found in the territory.

Seventeen miles beyond Whitehorse, travelers immerse themselves in the sweet and odorless mineral waters of Takhini Hot Springs. These sulfur-free springs are rumored to soothe a variety of aches and pains, and adjacent campsites give swimmers a place to relax after their soak. Back on the road, following the Takhini River, the Alaska Highway meets a side road leading south to emerald green Kusawa Lake. The first campsite along this 15-mile road offers access to the Takhini for fishing and boating. A second camping area, located at the end of the road, rests on the lakeshore.

This region reveals to travelers the area's volatile geological history. What appears to be thick layers of white sand is actually volcanic ash. More than a thousand years ago, an eruption in the southwest corner of the territory dumped sediment over an area greater than 100,000 square miles. Geologists believe the ash fell like a gentle snowfall, resulting in accumulations of a few inches to two feet. The ash can be seen here and there along the length of the Alaska Highway.

On the highway after the Kusawa Lake turnoff, signs warn drivers to watch for an unusual hazard: free-roaming bison. This is one of several places along the route where these animals graze on open range, in the full view—and sometimes the direct passage—of motorists.

As the highway continues west to Haines Junction, it goes through the Native community of Champagne. The village lies on one side of the road, a burial ground on the other. Champagne was established as a trading post around the turn of the century on the historic Dalton Trail. The trail was a popular route for prospectors coming from Haines, Alaska, over the ancient Chilkat Trail—a trade route established by Tlingit Natives—to the interior goldfields of the Klondike.

Aishihik Road offers another chance to stray from the main highway and enjoy the backcountry. Scenic Otter Falls, located 17 miles from the junction on Aishihik River, is pictured on the old Canadian five-dollar bill; now it is the site of a hydroelectric dam. At the southern end of Aishihik Lake is a territorial campground. Inspection of the gravel along the lakeshore may reveal a find of jasper or agate, both common in the area.

Pink fireweed brightens numerous spots along the roadway.

Returning to the Alaska Highway, the road crosses Aishihik River, known earlier as Canyon Creek. Just east of the new bridge is the old one-lane Canyon Creek bridge. The original structure, built around the turn of the century, was used to move supplies and people across the river from Silver City on Kluane Lake. Now it is a bit of history, providing highway travelers with a rare opportunity to see an original bridge.

Few sights are more spectacular than the first glimpse of the St. Elias Range. Named by explorer Vitus Bering, who first spotted the mountains on St. Elias Day in 1741, they include Mount Logan, the second highest peak in North America (Alaska's Mount McKinley is the tallest). Thousands of years of snowfalls in the range have created another vast phenomenon: the Kluane Icefields. From the highway, views of the St. Elias mountains are sometimes impeded by the Front Range. But travelers can obtain fuller looks at these imperious peaks just ahead, in Kluane National Park.

HAINES JUNCTION
TO ALASKA BORDER

LEFT: FLIGHTSEEING LENDS AN EXTRA DIMENSION TO THE TRAVELER'S ENJOYMENT OF KLUANE NATIONAL PARK.

RIGHT: LARGE BEARS MAY GET MOST OF THE ATTENTION, BUT SMALL CREATURES SUCH AS THIS GROUND SQUIRREL ALSO MAKE ROADSIDE APPEARANCES.

Haines Junction bustles beneath the imposing silhouette of the St. Elias Range. Like many communities along the highway, this one originated as a construction site, and it continues to welcome visitors. Tourism dominates its economy, and streams of sightseers converge upon the town each summer. Many come in search of high adventure in the backcountry of Kluane National Park, Canada's largest. Seventy-five percent of the town's 500 residents are employed in the park's spectacular wilderness setting. Both the headquarters and visitors' center for the park are located in Haines Junction.

Kluane National Park is virtually undeveloped, lacking any major road access. Its only campground is located 15 miles down the Haines Highway, at crystalline Kathleen Lake, and the campsites were designed to be as unobtrusive as possible. Trails wind through the mountains and lush valleys, over expanses of tundra and across ancient lake beds, often within sight of the magnificent St. Elias. Anglers can also find adventure. Fish include rainbow and lake trout, and Kokanee, a landlocked salmon species.

One of the least used but most exciting ways to explore the park is by floatplane. Local air taxi services will fly visitors to isolated lakes, picking them up later at a designated time. Or scenic one-hour flights will take travelers over mountain ranges, providing a new perspective of the awesome topography of the land.

For some, travel along the Alaska Highway begins 150 miles beyond the park, in the Alaska seaport of Haines. Those who traveled the Inside Passage on the Alaska State Ferry System disembark here to join the highway. But no matter where you start your journey on the road, the experience offers endless surprises. As the drive ventures north, the landscape undergoes a pronounced change. Moist air from the Pacific Coast is blocked by high mountain ranges, and harsher arctic influences begin to take hold. Trees diminish in variety, number, and size, and the slow-growing black spruce becomes dominant.

Another noticeable change is the condition of the highway. Permafrost, heavy traffic, and extremes in temperature begin to play havoc with the road. Seasonal changes cause surfaces to expand and contract, sometimes heaving sections up or down. Motorists' terms for these sudden disruptions range from the affectionate "whoop-de-dos" to decidedly more hostile expressions.

Spectacular sights become routine as the road winds through the Front Range of the St. Elias. Boutillier Summit, at 3,293 feet, offers the first glimpse of shimmering Kluane Lake. On a clear day the lake's waters reflect intense color, often a turquoise blue. The largest lake in the Yukon, Kluane measures approximately 40 miles long and between two and six miles wide.

A three-mile side trip off the highway provides the traveler with another periscope to the past. Silver City, once a prosperous mining community, now lies in tattered ruins. Ghostly remains consist of an old trading post, a roadhouse, and North West Mounted Police barracks. At the height of its fame around the turn of the century, Silver City was the lake's southern gateway for stampeders.

Next, the road dips to the shores of the lake and crosses Slim's River bridge. Slim's River is fed by the Kaskawulsh Glacier. A well-maintained trail cuts through the valley from the road, offering pleasant day hikes or longer ventures to view the colossal stretch of ice that forms the glacier.

Hugging the shore of Kluane Lake, the road passes Sheep Mountain, named for the Dall sheep inhabiting its slopes. An interpretative center provides information about the sheep, other fauna, and the flora of Kluane National Park. The center also allows visitors an opportunity to catch a glimpse of the snowy white Dall sheep on the slopes through high-powered telescopes.

The interpretative center isn't the only vantage point for seeing the sheep. Neighboring campgrounds on the shores of Kluane Lake also make excellent lookout points, as well as first-rate fishing sites.

MALE DALL SHEEP SPORT
MAGNIFICENT, SPIRALLING HORNS.

A recreational jewel lies tucked in the southwest corner of the Yukon Territory. Covering over 5,400,000 acres, Kluane National Park is the biggest park in Canada, but its fame is not limited to the North. In 1980 the United Nations designated it a World Heritage Site, along with its neighbor, the Wrangell–St. Elias National Park and Preserve in Alaska. The Wrangell–St. Elias mountain ranges—sharing a common ecologic and geologic heritage—dominate both areas.

Peaks within Kluane National Park include Mount Logan, the country's highest at 19,850 feet. Thirty-five others top 15,000 feet. Mountains here are among the continent's youngest and most active, with faults averaging 1,000 tremors a year. The Wrangell–St. Elias ranges possess the most extensive array of glaciers and ice fields found outside the polar regions.

A rich habitat surrounds Kluane's icy center, supporting a wide variety of life. A Native village on the Klushu Creek may be the oldest settlement in the Yukon. Coastal, arctic, mountain, and northern prairie vegetation intermingle here. Valley floors are lush grasslands sprouting rare specimens such as pasture sagewort, bluegrass, and wheatgrass. Alpine meadows feature brightly colored arctic poppies, while willow and dwarf birch provide protection for the fragile tundra. The park is home to many species of animals, and has the world's greatest population of Dall sheep—around 4,000. Over 150 species of birds have been identified.

Since Kluane is a wilderness area with no road access, it can only really be enjoyed and explored on foot. Hikers of all experience levels will find trails to match their skills. A short walk along Rock Glacier Trail reveals a wide valley flanked by rocky glaciers. Overnight treks, including a two-day venture to the Kaskawulsh Glacier, take backpackers to spectacular rivers of ice and countless small lakes.

(Kluane is the Indian word for "place of many fish," and frequently lives up to its promise.) Lake trout weighing 50 pounds or more, wily northern pike, and grayling inhabit the waters. Along the lakeshore, rockhounds will find an abundant supply of red jasper pebbles.

Directly across the road from the Sheep Mountain Visitors Center is Soldier's Summit. A sign commemorates the official opening of the highway here on November 20, 1942. Nearby is another historically significant site, Burwash Landing. The landing furnished supplies to miners working nearby streams, and gold is still found along Burwash Creek. Most of the community's population is Tutchone Indian, an Athapaskan group. The excellent Kluane Natural History Museum offers informative exhibits tracing both their ancestry and that of the later settlers, as well as displays on animals indigenous to the region and local rock and mineral specimens.

Leaving the shores of Kluane Lake, travelers are reminded of another of nature's great forces. Glacial drift, a remnant of the last ice age, dominates the topography, feeding massive rivers such as the Donjek and White. Great clouds of dust make their way down the rivers' valleys, as winds whip up the fine glacial silt. Donjek derives from an Indian word: donyak is a highly nutritious peavine that grows in the valley, providing food for game and stock. The White River was named for the glacial silt suspended in its waters.

The highway now traverses a lowland area characterized by numerous small lakes and ponds. A dirt road leads off the highway to a small campsite and abandoned Native village. Once part of the route prospectors took from the northern to the southern goldfields, the area is now notable because the lowest temperature recorded in Canada—81 degrees below zero—occurred here.

Beaver Creek is the last Canadian outpost on the highway, and the former site of Canadian customs at the Alaska border. The Canadian portion of the highway was unofficially connected to the Alaskan segment here in October 1942. The local visitors' center has a pictorial display about the construction period.

Leaving the Yukon, some travelers experience a sense of loss. Has the true wilderness come to an end? But that feeling quickly departs in Alaska. There are no boundaries for the spirit of the North.

TOP: SCULLY, A BURL CARVER AT KLUANE WILDERNESS VILLAGE, CLAIMS HE GETS A BETTER GRIP WHEN BAREFOOTED.

BOTTOM: ITS ECLECTIC ARRAY OF ODDS AND ENDS MAKES THIS LODGE TOO INTRIGUING TO IGNORE.

RIGHT: BY SUNSET, MOST MOTORISTS HAVE RETIRED TO THE CAMPFIRE, TRANSFORMING HIGHWAY TRAVEL INTO A SOLITARY JOY.

PORT ALCAN
CHISANA
MCCARTHY
NORTHWAY
TETLIN
TOK
TANACROSS
DOT LAKE
DELTA JUNCTION

MIDWAY LAKE
QUARTZ LAKE

LEFT: VAST STRETCHES OF ALASKA ARE INACCESSIBLE BY ROAD, MAKING FLOATPLANES POPULAR.
ABOVE: HOMESTEADER MARY HANSEN, OF DELTA JUNCTION, WAS ONE OF THE FIRST WOMEN SLED DOG RACERS IN ALASKA.

laska is a land that defies superlatives, daunting in almost any aspect. One-fifth the size of the Lower 48 contiguous states, its 500,000 square miles encompass at least three million lakes and 5,000 glaciers. The state is home to the continent's highest peak, 20,320-foot Mount McKinley, and its biggest land mammal, the grizzly bear. In the state's Matanuska Valley, even the cabbages reach record size, weighing as much as 80 pounds.

The mystique of Alaska, called The Great Land by the Natives, is also larger than life. First enticed by opportunity, many visitors find themselves entranced by beauty, unable to leave. While hardships are also plentiful in this harsh landscape, Alaska's challenges inspire accomplishment, forging bonds with the country as strong as steel. Even the empty-handed prospector took home the strength of experience and a renewed belief in his own powers.

Alaska's people are as diverse as its features. The Natives, the state's first inhabitants, make up 13 percent of its population, or around 65,000 people. They are frequently characterized as belonging to three main groups: Eskimo, Aleut, and Indian, including the Athapaskan and Tlingit. Many lead subsistence lifestyles, following the traditions laid down by generations of ancestors. Others are physicians, teachers, and legislators. All play roles in the evolution

of the state. In 1971, as part of the landmark Alaska Native Claims Settlement Act, the state's Natives received both land and money. Thirteen regional corporations were created to manage the settlement.

With Alaska's other residents, Natives share an appreciation of the state's eccentricities and uniqueness. So great is this universal sense of independence that Alaskans refer to the rest of the world as a single unit: Outside.

One-half of Alaska's half-million people live in Anchorage. The rest are scattered across the far reaches of the state, mostly in bush communities. Defined as any area not accessible by road, the geographic area represented by the bush is staggering. Not surprisingly, airplanes are a common mode of travel. Alaska's per capita ownership of planes is the nation's highest.

Large sections of Alaska remain remote, but the visitor will find much of interest within easy access. A number of federal, state, and local parks can be reached by roadways. And Alaska's prolific wildlife population doesn't observe boundaries. Motorists are likely to encounter such common species as black bear, moose, and snowshoe hare, especially in the evening. During their migrations, caribou appear by the thousands along the roadways. In the fall, the distant sounds of Canada geese are heard just before daybreak as they gather to head south.

Scenic splendor is Alaska's proudest attribute, but its economic base is oil. Eighty-five percent of the state's revenues come from this industry. Just outside of Delta Junction at the official end of the highway, visitors get their first look at the 800-mile-long trans-Alaska pipeline that carries crude oil from the North Slope of the state to Valdez in the south. Alaska also possesses vast reserves of natural gas.

From earliest times, Alaska's sheer enormity tantalized outsiders. They often left the region with riches, and were convinced its bounty would never be depleted. Now Alaska is recognized as a fragile place, its resources just as exhaustible as those found in the Lower 48. Travelers will quickly sense they are in the presence not of an invulnerable force, but an unspeakably rare flower, one of the last great natural landscapes on earth.

OVERLEAF: THIS SITE SOUTH OF NORTHWAY JUNCTION IS ONE OF MANY OFFERING INCOMPARABLE VIEWS OF AUTUMN COLORS.

ABOVE: THE MASSIVE TRANS-ALASKA PIPELINE FIRST APPEARS ALONG THE HIGHWAY JUST WEST OF DELTA JUNCTION, WHERE IT CROSSES THE TANANA RIVER.

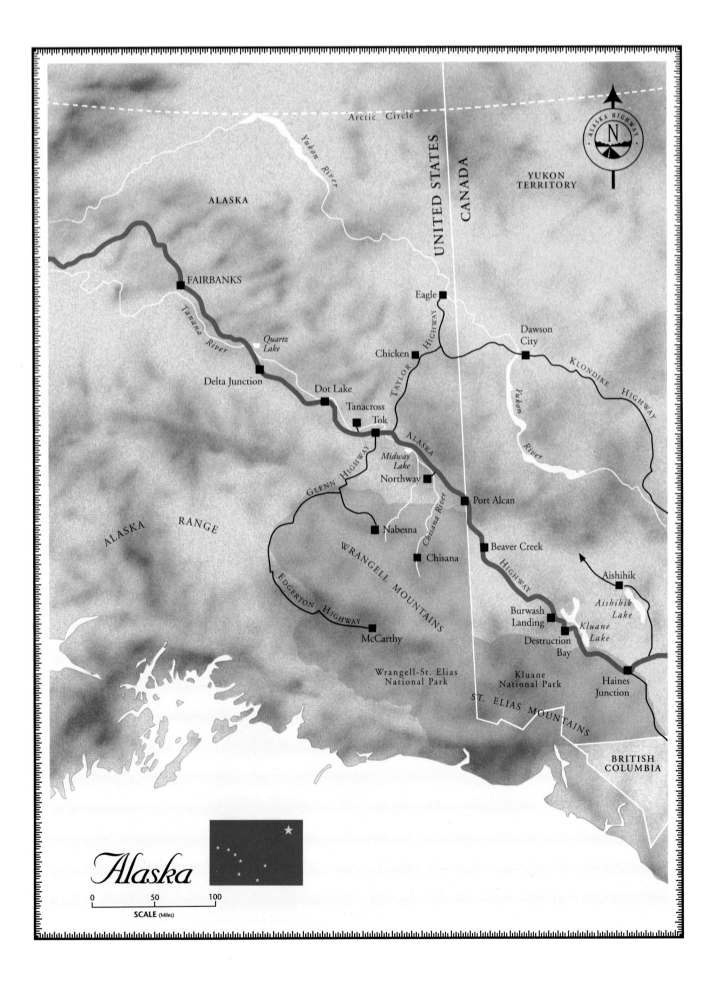

Arctic Circle

N
ALASKA HIGHWAY

YUKON
TERRITORY

UNITED STATES
CANADA

ALASKA

Yukon River

FAIRBANKS

Tanana River

Quartz Lake

Delta Junction

Dot Lake

Tanacross

Tok

Eagle

Chicken

TAYLOR HIGHWAY

Dawson City

KLONDIKE HIGHWAY

Yukon River

Midway Lake

Northway

ALASKA

Nabesna

Chisana River

Chisana

Port Alcan

GLENN HIGHWAY

ALASKA RANGE

WRANGELL MOUNTAINS

EDGERTON HIGHWAY

McCarthy

Wrangell-St. Elias
National Park

Beaver Creek

HIGHWAY

Aishihik

Aishihik Lake

Burwash
Landing

Kluane Lake

Destruction
Bay

Kluane
National Park

Haines
Junction

ST. ELIAS MOUNTAINS

BRITISH
COLUMBIA

Alaska

SCALE (Miles)
0   50   100

ALASKA BORDER
TO TOK

LEFT: A MAJESTIC TRUMPETER
SWAN FLOATS ON A LAKE
NEAR THE CANADIAN BORDER,
FOLLOWED BY A SMALL
PROCESSION OF DUCKS.
RIGHT: THIS SIGN MARKS THE
TOK VISITOR INFORMATION
CENTER, WHERE DISPLAYS
ABOUT ALASKA'S HISTORY AND
WILDLIFE GREET TRAVELERS.

ummer is the busiest time at Port Alcan, the U.S. customs station on the Alaska border. About 25 people make their home in this tiny community. Passage through the checkpoint is usually smooth, but sometimes circumstances trigger a logjam of automobiles. At the start of the tourist season or during economic boom times, autos crowd the familiar portal. Many go south after the arrival of the Permanent Fund dividend checks. Based on Alaska's oil earnings, these annual payments are given to every resident man, woman, and child. In recent years, checks have averaged around $800, and many Alaskans like to spend the bonus Outside.

Beyond Port Alcan, the road nudges the eastern interior of the state. Massive mountain ranges lie to the west, including the Wrangell–St. Elias and the Mentasta. As the road makes a gradual descent, elevation averages 1,500 feet. For the next 65 miles, the highway parallels the magnificent Tetlin Wildlife Refuge, a habitat of one million square miles. This protected sanctuary lies in the path of a major north-south flyway for migratory waterfowl and other birds. Each spring, half of the world's population of sandhill cranes, about 200,000, arrive at the refuge to breed over the summer. Also common are trumpeter swans, loons, bald and golden eagles, ptarmigan (Alaska's state bird), and the state's largest population of osprey. The

ABOVE: POPPIES AND OTHER
BRIGHT SUMMER WILDFLOWERS
ACCENT THE ROADSIDE.
BELOW: MIDWAY LAKE
SHIMMERS BENEATH THE
TOWERING WRANGELL
MOUNTAINS.

refuge is one of 16 in the state and is part of a national system of protected lands.

South of the refuge is another magnificent area, the Wrangell–St. Elias Park and Preserve. The preserve borders the Yukon's Kluane National Park, and together the two make up a nearly impregnable region of 12 million square acres that doesn't easily submit to exploration by even the most determined hiker. Those who succeed find a majesty comparable to that of the Himalayas and the Andes. Four of the park's peaks top 16,000 feet— at just over 18,000, Mount St. Elias is the tallest—and attract expert mountaineers from all over the world. A land of perpetual snow, the park contains over 150 glaciers, and has been described as the sole surviving example of the forbidding world of the ice age.

Only a handful of settlements exists on the fringes of these formidable mountains. Residents carry on the occupations of their predecessors—prospector, trapper, and guide. Chisana, located at the head of the scenic Chisana River valley, is one of two permanent communities remaining in the Wrangell Mountains. McCarthy is the other. The discovery of gold in the valley resulted in the first European settlement, in 1913. Flushed with Yukon fever, many prospectors never realized they had crossed the border of Canada into Alaska.

ATHAPASKAN CHIEF ANDREW ISAAC, SHOWN HERE IN JULY 1990,
PROUDLY DISPLAYS HIS CEREMONIAL DRESS.

the starving men back to health.

In the old times, that's the way it was, Northway recalls. "When you saw someone in need, you helped them." Northway is the traditional chief of a small Athapaskan village that bears his name. Most of the residents are related. Northway has seen many things change since that day, around the turn of the century, when he first saw the white men. His people's hunting and fishing lifestyle has been replaced by a cash economy. Undaunted, Northway continues to teach the new generations the values of their ancestors.

Andrew Isaac, who was traditional chief of the Athapaskans of Interior Alaska until he died in 1991 at the age of 93, was also concerned about preserving the old ways. He worried that the culture he cherished would soon disappear. Isaac remembered that his people never wasted anything from an animal they killed. "We took moose skin, cut a hole, and made a bed," he said. "We made clothes from caribou skin."

Today, fewer Athapaskans practice the old traditions. But as public demand for Native crafts increases, interest in these painstaking arts revives. All along the Alaska Highway, businesses sell Native creations. Bleached moosehide slippers are beaded with colorful floral designs and adorned in fur. Haunting figures are carved in stone. And from time to time, a lucky tourist may happen upon snowshoes handcrafted by Chief Walter Northway.

The first time Walter Northway saw a white man, he was 14 years old. He was walking near his home by the Chisana River when he heard strange-sounding voices. He ran back to the hunting camp where his father sat roasting ducks. Two haggard men followed him, their clothes frayed and torn. They were prospectors, and in the course of searching for the Chisana goldfields they had become lost. Northway's people nursed

Sand dunes formed by glacial debris line this stretch of highway. In the summer, fireweed, wild pink sweet pea, pale yellow Indian paintbrush, and bright yellow yarrow create a colorful roadside vision.

At Northway Junction, a side road leads back into the Tetlin Wildlife Refuge, culminating in the village of Northway. A Native community of around 350, the town was historically occupied by the Athapaskans. Residents supplement subsistence incomes with traditional handicrafts. Visitors to the area can purchase moccasins, birch-bark baskets, and Native boots (mukluks). The U.S. Customs Service checkpoint for small aircraft is also located in Northway, and the airport is a hub for a variety of recreational activities.

To the northwest, the Tanana River begins to parallel the highway. Before the roadway existed, the river was the main transportation route through the eastern interior. The largest Alaskan tributary of the Yukon, the Tanana is joined by two glacial streams, the Chisana and the Nabesna. Beautiful Midway Lake can be seen from the road, but Tetlin, a small Native village, hides 10 miles inland in the flats.

At Tetlin Junction, the Taylor and Alaska highways meet. The Taylor's gravel road leads to the tiny pioneer settlements of Chicken and Eagle, then intersects the road to Dawson City, Yukon Territory. The vivacious center of the gold rush, Dawson for a brief time became one of North America's best-known cities. Thousands sought wealth in the nearby goldfields, their sagas celebrated by such writers as Jack London, Robert Service, and Rex Beach. Contemporary Dawson is more dignified than its ancestor, but there are many vivid reminders of that feisty past.

Next to Dawson, the nearest sizable community is Tok (pronounced Tōk). This Alaskan town of 1,600 takes tourism seriously: there are more lodges and restaurants per capita here than anyplace else in the state. Visitors will enjoy freshly baked salmon, sourdough pancakes, and reindeer sausage.

Tourism isn't the only serious business in Tok. The town is unofficially known as the "Sled Dog Capital of Alaska," a center for breeding, training, and mushing. Information about Alaska's favorite sport is available on the highway at the headquarters of the Tok Dog Mushers Association. Mushing passion peaks during the Iditarod Trail Sled Dog Race, the great 1,100-mile trek from Anchorage to Nome that occurs in March every year, but the Iditarod is just one of many races that take place throughout Alaska all winter.

LEFT: MOOSE FORAGE AT NUMEROUS SPOTS ALONG NORTH COUNTRY ROADSIDES. *ABOVE:* A SLED DOG RACER PRAISES HIS ANIMAL FOLLOWING A BRACING RUN. MUSHING IS ALASKA'S OFFICIAL STATE SPORT.

TOK TO
DELTA JUNCTION

Colorful wood houses decorate a small Tanah Native settlement in the shadow of the Alaska Range. The Old Eagle Trail crossed the Tanana River here, resulting in the village's name, Tanacross. The town of 100 boasts an unlikely asset: an airstrip with two 5,000-foot runways. The airstrip is used primarily as a base for firefighting operations. In the summer, the strip is transformed into a speedway, and stock cars zoom down the runways during local races. The village also sponsors other contests. On Memorial Day and Labor Day, boats churn between Tanacross and the Tanana River bridge, on the east side of Tok.

LEFT: DOT LAKE IS TYPICAL OF SERENE LANDSCAPES FOUND THROUGHOUT ALASKA.
RIGHT: DRIVERS NEAR DELTA JUNCTION MAY HAVE TO YIELD TO UNEXPECTED FELLOW VOYAGERS—BISON.

Another Athapaskan community is Dot Lake, located halfway between Tok and Delta Junction. Here travelers may chance upon a potlatch. Native people hold potlatches as a traditional way to celebrate significant life events, and the custom is a cultural touchstone of many Native American groups. In the course of the ceremony, traditional dancing and music take place and gifts are given to the guests.

Visitors to this stretch of highway are often surprised to discover the existence of extensive fields of barley. Alaska has long tried to encourage agriculture within its borders, and the Delta Barley Project is among these efforts. The state opened 65,000 acres here for farming, distributing them through a lottery in 1978. Barley was selected as the main crop because it

Above: This Alaskan takes a dim view of unsolicited correspondence.

Below: Thriving grain farms—some as large as 2,000 acres—fill the countryside outside Delta Junction.

suited the area's flat terrain and is hardy enough for the region's climate. Lesser quantities of oats and wheat are also planted.

It is a misconception that all of Alaska's soil is inhospitable to agriculture. Other factors have stymied farming in the state, such as the lack of major markets and processing plants. Wildlife sometimes destroys crops; a migrating herd of 400 bison, descendants from a Montana group shipped up in the 1920s, often meanders into fields and does considerable damage. Extreme cold is of course another deterrent. Temperatures routinely dip to between minus 60 and minus 80 degrees Fahrenheit in the winter. In that frigid environment, a tossed cup of coffee freezes in midair, like a small dark cloud.

Just outside Delta Junction, Clearwater Road cuts a swath through pastoral countryside to the Clearwater State Recreation Site, one of the best fishing spots in the Interior. Fly fishermen's lines loop in the search for arctic grayling that inhabit the spring-fed Clearwater River. More difficult to land are the round whitefish native to the river. Each October, silver salmon journey up river for their annual spawn.

helped pioneer glacier landings, opening approaches for mountaineers. Don Sheldon's daring mountain rescue flights are the stuff of legend.

Of course, harrowing midflight adventure is not the goal of most tourists. With the development of sophisticated technology, Alaska bush flying is a safe experience today. Planes now are heated and comfortable, letting passengers relax and savor the marvels of this type of travel. Local air taxi operations provide a variety of services and expertise. Floatplanes ferry hikers and anglers to remote lakes and rivers, or leave campers for an unparalleled week of solitude. Even an hour of flightseeing is exhilarating, revealing new aspects of the landscape. Flying over the immense topography of a mountain peak adds a new chapter to the traveler's notebook.

MOON LAKE—NORTH OF TOK—IS A POPULAR DOCKING SITE FOR FLOATPLANES.

The bush pilot remains one of the North Country's most romantic images. Since the mid-1920s, this special breed of aviator has helped chart the remote reaches of Alaska and northern Canada. Over time, bush pilots have become indispensable. Without them, essentials such as medical care, mail, and fresh produce would be infrequent in vast parts of Alaska.

Part local hero, part freewheeling stuntman, the bush pilot functions in a climate of extreme unpredictability. Cold temperatures, clouds, and winds create menacing flying conditions. Unscheduled wilderness landings may be triumphs of ingenuity over good sense. Despite the hazards, the list of legendary figures is long. Noel Wien developed widespread cargo routes starting in the late 1920s. Bob Reeve

RIGHT: RIKA'S ROADHOUSE—
NOW ON THE NATIONAL
REGISTER OF HISTORIC
PLACES—CARRIES VISITORS
BACK IN TIME.
BELOW: SPRING AND SUMMER
AREN'T THE ONLY SEASONS
PROMISING GLIMPSES OF
WILDLIFE, AS THIS WINTER
SIGHTING OF A COYOTE PROVES.
FACING PAGE: NO LONGER
TREACHEROUS, THE ALASKA
HIGHWAY IS NOW AN
ENCHANTING PATHWAY
THROUGH SOME OF THE EARTH'S
LAST GREAT WILDERNESS.

Prior to construction of the Tanana River bridge, a ferry offered passage across the river. On the south bank is Rika's Roadhouse, one of the most attractive lodges in Alaska. A beacon to early travelers, it provided modest accommodations and food, plus supplies for horses and sled dogs. Roadhouses were common in the state before the highway was built, and they were generally run by a family. Spaced about a day's journey apart, they were centers of conversation and conviviality, a haven from the cold. Rika's has been restored and is on the National Register of Historic Places. A log cabin with a sod roof is among the displays, which include artifacts from the Athapaskans and the pioneers. The restaurant is still in operation. Rika's no longer offers overnight accommodations, but Quartz Lake State Recreation Area, on the north side of the Tanana, permits camping and freshwater fishing.

Milepost Marker 1422, in front of the Visitors Information Center in Delta Junction, designates the official end of the Alaska Highway. But this is not the end of the road. Most travelers will continue on by way of other thoroughfares, heading north to Fairbanks, or south to Valdez and Anchorage. Within a few weeks, perhaps a few months, travelers can retrace their paths back down the highway. Now veterans, they have a second chance to experience the trip, recapturing the marvels of the first great road through the northern wilderness—the historic Alaska Highway.

Reading List

Brebner, Phyllis Lee. *The Alaska Highway: A Personal & Historical Account of the Building of the Alaska Highway*. Erin, Ont.: Boston Mills Press, 1985.

Brown, Earl, photography, and Lyn Hancock, text. *Alaska Highway, Road to Adventure*. Fort Nelson, B.C.: Autumn Images, 1988.

Callison, Pat. *Pack Dogs to Helicopters: Pat Callison's Story*. Vancouver, B.C.: Evergreen Press, 1983.

Christy, Jim. *Rough Road to the North: Travels Along the Alaska Highway*. New York: Doubleday, 1980.

Cohen, Stan. *The Trail of '42: A Pictorial History of the Alaska Highway*. Missoula, Mont.: Pictorial Histories Publishing Co., 1990.

_____ . *The Forgotten War*, Vols. I and II, Missoula, Mont.: Pictorial Histories Publishing Co., 1988 and 1989, respectively.

Coutts, Robert. *Yukon Places and Names*. Vancouver, B.C.: Hancock House, 1980.

Dalby, Ron. *The Alaska Highway: An Insider's Guide*. Golden, Colo.: Fulcrum Publishing, 1991.

Davignon, Ellen. *The Cinnamon Mine: Memories of an Alaska Highway Childhood*. Altona, Manit.: D. W. Friesen and Sons Ltd., 1988.

Duncan, Allan. *Medicine, Madames, and Mounties: Stories of a Yukon Doctor, 1943 to 1947*. Vancouver, B.C.: Raincoast, 1989.

Henning, Robert, Ed. *Adventure Roads North: The Story of the Alaska Highway and Other Roads in the MILEPOST*. Anchorage: The Alaska Geographic Society, 1983.

Lerdahl, Herman, with Cliff Cernick. *Skystruck: True Tales of an Alaska Bush Pilot*. Bothell, Wash.: Alaska Northwest Books, 1989.

Morritt, Hope. *Land of the Fireweed: A Young Woman's Story of Alaska Highway Construction Days*. Edmonds, Wash.: Alaska Northwest Publishing Company, 1985.

Remley, David A. *Crooked Road: The Story of the Alaska Highway*. New York: McGraw-Hill Book Co., 1976.

Whitesitt, Larry L. *Flight of the Red Beaver: A Yukon Adventure*. Coeur d'Alene, Idaho: Century Publishing Company, 1990.

Whyard, Florence. *Canadian Bush Pilot: Ernie Boffa*. Anchorage: Alaska Northwest Publishing Company, 1984.

Woolcock, Iris. *The Road North: One Woman's Adventure Driving the Alaska Highway*. Anchorage: Greatland Graphics, 1990.

INDEX

ABOUT THE WRITER AND THE PHOTOGRAPHER

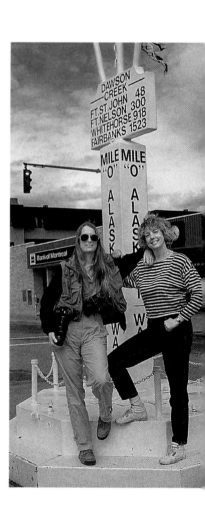

Photographer Alissa Crandall and writer Gloria J. Maschmeyer have received numerous awards for their work.

Alissa Crandall has been a published photographer for over 20 years. As a teenager, the California native sold prints to neighbors, and also had some of her first images included in the book *Early to Learn*. Crandall has lived in Alaska since 1977. Her photographs can be found in magazines, newspapers, and other publications, including *Alaska* magazine, *BBC Wildlife* magazine, the *Christian Science Monitor*, and Sierra Club calendars. She has also received recognition in the *Best of Photography Annual*, and her work is included in the collections of the Alaska State Arts Bank and the University of Alaska–Fairbanks Museum.

Gloria J. Maschmeyer's home base has been Anchorage for over ten years. Exotic locales have also furnished background for her writings. An ardent traveler, she has lived in Madrid and Singapore, where she served as an editor at APA Publications and as Asian correspondent for the travel magazine *Passages*. The rich personalities and special challenges of life in America's most remote state are the subject of much of Maschmeyer's work. She authored the Anchorage chapter in the travel book *Insight Guide Alaska* and revised and updated the latest edition. Her byline has appeared regularly in *Anchorage* magazine, and she authored a brochure, *Anchorage Highways*, for Alaska's Division of Tourism.

ALISSA CRANDALL, *LEFT*, AND GLORIA J. MASCHMEYER, *RIGHT*, AT MILE 0 ON THE ALASKA HIGHWAY.

ALASKA NORTHWEST BOOKS™

*offers many more intriguing books about
the North Country, including:*

The MILEPOST®, The ALASKA WILDERNESS MILEPOST®, and NORTHWEST MILEPOSTS®.

Since 1949, *The MILEPOST®* has served as the bible of North Country travel. Updated annually, this classic guide provides mile-by-mile information on what to see and do, and where to find food, gas, and lodging. It includes a fold-out "Plan-a-Trip" map and information on customs, air travel, hunting and fishing. Companion guides, *The ALASKA WILDERNESS MILEPOST®* and *NORTHWEST MILEPOSTS®*, round out the picture, with facts about over 250 remote towns and villages in Alaska, Washington, Oregon, Idaho, Montana, and southwestern Canada. With countless photos and maps.

The MILEPOST®/600 pages/softbound/$16.95($18.95 Canadian)/ISBN 0-88240-215-3

The ALASKA WILDERNESS MILEPOST®/450 pages/softbound/$14.95 ($18.95 Canadian)/
    ISBN 0-88240-290-0

NORTHWEST MILEPOSTS®/328 pages/softbound/$14.95 ($18.95 Canadian)/ISBN 088240-278-1

Facts About Alaska: The ALASKA ALMANAC®, *Fifteenth Edition*

Whether the subject is popular in nature—the Iditarod Trail Sled Dog Race, for instance—or matter of fact, you'll find the latest data, drawings, and maps to answer any questions about Alaska, America's Last Frontier. With 60 drawings, 20 maps.

245 pages/softbound/$8.95 ($10.95 Canadian)/ISBN 0-88240-248-X

Iditarod: The Great Race to Nome, *Photography by Jeff Schultz, Text by Bill Sherwonit*

This attractive book chronicles the spectacle of the longest sled dog race in the world: the 1,100-mile Iditarod. Introductory essays are provided by Susan Butcher, four-time champion, and Joe Redington, Sr., often called the "father" of the contest and still competing at age 73. With 80 color photographs, 20 historical photos, 5 maps.

144 page/softbound/$19.95 ($24.95 Canadian)/ISBN 0-88240-411-3

Shamans and Kushtakas: North Coast Tales of the Supernatural,

by Mary Giraudo Beck, Illustrated by Martin Oliver

History and legend mingle in this powerful look at the values and traditions of the Tlingit and Haida societies in Southeast Alaska. The book's tales provide lively adventure reading for old and young. With 9 drawings.

128 pages/softbound/$12.95 ($15.95 Canadian)/ISBN 0-88240-406-7

Ask for these books at your favorite bookstore, or contact Alaska Northwest Books™ for a catalog of our entire list.

Alaska Northwest Books™
A division of GTE Discovery Publications, Inc.
P.O. Box 3007
Bothell, WA 98041-3007
Toll free 1-800-343-4567